Bake

Guide &

Lindsey Porter

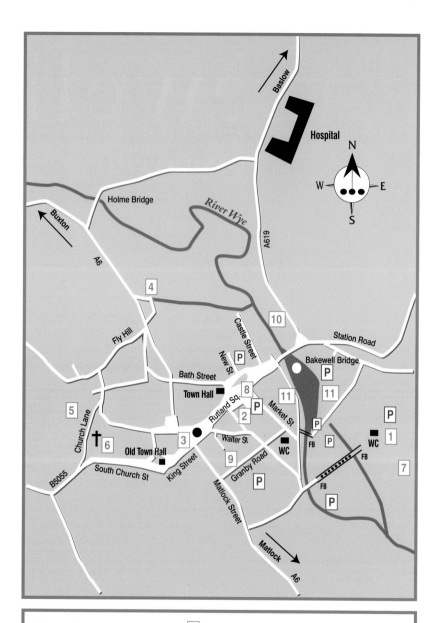

Bakewell

FB = Footbridge

1   Agricultural Centre

2   Portland Shopping Centre

3   Rutland Hotel

4   Victoria Mill

5   Old House Museum

6   All Saints Church

7   Bakewell Show Site

8   Market Hall

9   Library, Swimming Pool, TIC

10 Scotts Garden

11 Riverside Walk

Bakewell

Above: Bakewell Bridge
Below: The Bath House

Most National Parks outside this country are largely devoid of much habitation by man. Here in the middle of the Peak District National Park sits the town of Bakewell! Its church is thought to have a Saxon foundation and in its churchyard are two Saxon crosses, one standing eight feet high and probably dating from the end of the 8th century.

Bakewell sits on the banks of the River Wye and developed as a crossing of the river. Its market dates from 1254 and its ancient bridge was built about 50 years later. The town retains its cattle market having been rebuilt a few years ago on a new site across the river. Despite recent development, most of which has been outside the old town, it still retains considerable charm.

(Image Courtesy of www.visitpeakdistrict.com)

In fact Bakewell is very popular with its visitors and has been that way for centuries. The well travelled diarist, Celia Fiennes came through the town in 1697, describing it as a 'pretty neate market town' and it remains so. Numerous shops hidden away in small side streets and courtyards serve local needs and those of tourists. Quality clothes, handcrafted jewellery, original artwork, camping and outdoor specialists, Bakewell puddings and a Farmer's Market shop are a few. A new Agricultural Centre incorporating the cattle market (held every Monday) was built on the east side of the river, clearing the way for a development from the Market Hall area to the river on the west bank. The project includes shops, housing, a new swimming pool and a supermarket. Developments have been carefully planned to retain the atmosphere of a 'neate town'.

Just beyond the shops is the River Wye, its crystal clear waters the home of numerous large and lazy fish that know the value of tasty morsels thrown in for ducks and fish alike. The riverside walk, even just the section downstream from the ancient bridge, is very popular and the view to the bridge is particularly memorable when the daffodils are in flower.

The area of Rutland Square was set out by the Duke of Rutland to try and capitalise on the development of Buxton and Matlock as spa towns. Although this was a lost cause, in a sense, Bakewell had no need to worry. The visitors came anyway and their successors come here each year, by coach or car, on foot or bike. However, you arrive: **Welcome to Bakewell**.

A Tour of the Town

Start from the **Rutland Arms Hotel**. The adjacent Rutland Square was set out by the Duke of Rutland (the owner of nearby Haddon Hall and its estate) at the beginning of the nineteenth century, the hotel being constructed on its west side in 1804. On the north side of the square (just across from the hotel) is the former hotel stable block.

Adjacent to it is **Bath Gardens** set out with lawns and flowerbeds. It used to be the garden of Bath House, built in 1697 and situated at the end of Bath Street. This is now the home of the local branch of the British Legion, but was once the town house of the Duke of Rutland.

In its cellar a huge bath remains that was built for the Duke. Spa water filled it, but whether it was as warm and therapeutic as the facilities at Buxton is not clear. One of the town's well dressing frames is erected at the rear of Bath House on the last Saturday in June. It is always very impressive and probably the town's largest well dressing.

Rutland Arms Hotel

From **Rutland Square**, walk up King Street (left hand side of the hotel). At the end of the block on the right hand side is the former **Old Town Hall**. This small but elegant building stands back from the road with a large forecourt. It dates from 1602 and has had a succession of uses. The Old Town Hall was on the first floor, with the St John's Hospital on the ground floor.

Above Right: Victoria Mill

Above left: View near All Saints Church

Left: Bakewell Fruit & Flowers Shop

Below: Old Town Hall

In 1709, it was altered and almshouses were built behind it. Subsequent uses even included housing the town's fire engine! Passing in front of the old Town Hall you reach the churchyard and **The Church of All Saints**. Before taking this route, if you continue up the street to South Church Street, the last house on the right before the lane running back towards the church is the old school. It was built in 1636 and is the original home of Lady Manner's School, one of the oldest surviving schools in the county. The current school is on a large site above the town off the road to Monyash.

Above Left: Saxon Cross
Above Right: Saxon carved stones
Right: Monument to Sir John and Lady Manners
Below: The Norman arch and south transept

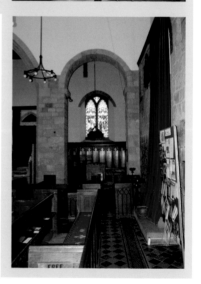

Bakewell Church is an elegant building situated high above the old town and with its high, 1840s steeple, completely dominates the townscape. Much of the early elements of the structure are Norman, but the Norman arch piercing the wall between the nave and south aisle is thought to be in a Saxon structure. The west front of the church dates from the twelfth century, its large window (set between two Norman arches) helping to flood the building with light.

It had been allowed to seriously deteriorate like many churches in Victorian times. The Octagon between the nave and chancel roofs, its supporting walls and the south aisle were re-built in the 1840s, the Octagon being used as the base of a graceful spire.

During the reconstruction of 1842-43, many carved stones were found of Saxon and Norman age. A lot of them were in the Octagon. Clearly some of these must have been stones reused from the earlier Saxon church. Fortunately, many were kept and stacked in the south porch and on the inside of the west front. There are lots of them! In fact it's the largest collection of stones of this age anywhere in the United Kingdom. Thank goodness for Victorian interest in 'antiquities', as they put it.

The south transept of Bakewell church is known as The Newark. It has several monuments that date from the 15th-17th century. However, what is particularly important is the wall-mounted one on your left as you approach the door into the south transept. It is of Sir Godfrey Foljambe and his wife and is in alabaster with coats of arms above. It dates from the 14th century and is understood (according to Pevsner's "Buildings of England: Derbyshire") to be the only surviving medieval example of a type of wall-monument popular from the (much later) 16th century. He describes it as being 'an internationally remarkable monument'.

This is a large and elegant church, well worth the visit.

Another nearby place well worth the visit is conveniently situated behind the church. It is the **Old House Museum** and was built as a parsonage house in 1543 and some 250 years later converted to a tenement house by Sir Richard Arkwright. After suffering years of neglect, the building was rescued by Bakewell Historical Society and painstakingly restored. It is open to the public with a blacksmith's, wheelwright's shop and a mill worker's dwelling house.

North Church Street and Church Lane (to the north and west of the church respectively) come together adjacent to Bagshaw Hill which leads past **Bagshaw Hall**, built in 1684. Bagshaw Hill leads down to Buxton road (A6). Turning to the left here, the road passes **Victoria Mill**, its huge waterwheel now resting and rusting away in the mill-yard. Further up the road, past the fire station, a path on the right leads to **Holme Bridge**. An interpretation board here describes the various watercourses built to serve Lumford and Victoria Mills. An old sheepwash can be seen beyond the sign.

The bridge is an old, narrow packhorse bridge, dating from 1664. It leads into Holme Lane. Opposite Burre House (about halfway down it from the bridge), there is a footpath through delightful river meadows known in part as Scott's Garden. It leads back to the main bridge and Bridge Street. Taking a right turn over the river, on the medieval road bridge built in 1300, brings you back into town. Look out for the **Old Market Hall** that dates from the early seventeenth century and is now the **Tourist Information Centre**, jointly operated by the Peak National Park Authority and Derbyshire Dales District Council. It has a comprehensive collection of information on the area as well as exhibitions and is well worth a visit. Here one can walk back

Bakewell Pudding

The Old Original Bakewell Pudding Shop
(*Image Courtesy of www.visitpeakdistrict.com*)

Several shops in Bakewell sell Bakewell Puddings, preserving the memory of the culinary accident that produced a new dish. The accident apparently occurred at the White Horse Inn (now the Rutland Arms) when a maid deputising for the cook was asked to make a strawberry tart. She spread the egg mixture on top of the jam instead of (as was usual) into the pastry. The guests were delighted and a local speciality was born.

Holme Bridge

along the street and into the centre of the town again. Alternatively, the riverside walk can be taken below the bridge, but this time on the opposite and west side of the river.

Close to Holme Bridge, with access off Holme Lane was a Chert Mine, now closed. This is a silicious material found in limestone beds. It is the same as flint that is found in chalk, but in nodules rather than in beds. Of great hardness, it was used for grinding bones and flints in the pottery industry in Stoke-on-Trent. So important was it, that the Bakewell, Leek, Stoke road was turnpiked to ease its transportation. An important sponsor and shareholder in this turnpike trust was Josiah Wedgwood.

Events in the Town

Bakewell Show

Bakewell Agricultural Show is a major event attracting around 65,000 each year. It is held on the first Wednesday and Thursday in August, adjacent to the cattle market, east of the river. It used to be the largest one-day show in the country, but such was its popularity it was decided to hold a two-day event.

The show features all aspects of farming and rural life, from the best of British livestock to the latest business and technological innovations.

There are show jumping competitions, a premier-status dog show, food, flowers, crafts, country pursuits, in fact something for the whole family to enjoy. Do allow a whole day.

☎ 01629 812736 Email: info@bakewellshow.org

Heavy Horse Turnabout, Bakewell Show

Cattle Judging, Bakewell Show

Cattle Judging, Bakewell Show

Images Courtesy of
www.bakewellshow.org

Left: Premier dog show, Bakewell Show

Below: Double Harness Surry Driving, Bakewell Show

Images Courtesy of
www.bakewellshow.org

Bakewell Arts Festival

This event takes place the weekend after Bakewell Show and offers music, theatre, poetry, exhibitions and workshops staged at various venues around the town.

Other country shows and fairs are held at nearby Chatsworth House. See their website www.chatsworth.org or telephone ☎ 01246 582204.

Well Dressing

Each year, the town joins in the annual well dressing ceremonies held across the Peak District. However, Bakewell was dressing its wells in the 18th century, but the event ceased before 1800. The custom was revived in 1971 and on the last Saturday in June the well dressings are erected and blessed on the following day. Four wells are dressed, two of them are in Bath Gardens and another is at the Butter Market in King Street. A more recent addition is the fourth, at Church Alley off South Church Street. The one at the rear of Bath House in Bath Gardens is generally

Bakewell Well Dressing
(*Above image courtesy of*
www.visitpeakdistrict.com)

particularly fine; one of the best anywhere in fact.

The tradition of well dressing is mainly a Derbyshire one. Wooden frames are filled with wet clay and flower petals, seeds, cones, leaves and shells are applied to create a scene. In 1977, two dressings from Bakewell were exhibited at the Chelsea Flower Show.

Bakewell Carnival

Well Dressing week ends with the Carnival on Saturday. A procession of floats and bands parade through the main streets ending with a fete in the Recreation Ground. Various other events take place during this week including a raft race on the River Wye. This is usually held on Thursday (weather permitting) and the best place to watch it is the old bridge in Bridge Street, but arrive early!

www.bakewellcarnival.co.uk

Exploring around Bakewell

Bakewell is a good centre for exploring the mid-Peak District area. Nearby are Chatsworth House – the Palace of the Peak, Haddon Hall, a short distance from town on the A6 and Lathkill Dale within a site of special scientific interest, with crystal-clear waters of the River Lathkill. All are quite close and well worth a visit.

Chatsworth House

Getting there: take the Baslow road over the old bridge in the middle part of the town. After a couple of miles or so, turn right for Pilsley. Look out for the Chatsworth Farmshop on the right. In addition to good quality produce, there is a tea room/restaurant at the rear, with good views across the estate. Continue on to the T-junction and turn right for Edensor village and Chatsworth.

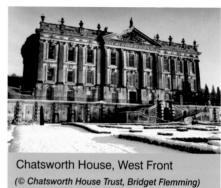

Chatsworth House, West Front
(© Chatsworth House Trust, Bridget Flemming)

Edensor village was moved from the area of the main road in the 1840s. All the properties are different. Traditionally, the duke was given various designs and was unable to choose one, so he decided to have one of each. In the churchyard is the grave of Joseph Paxton, who built the Crystal Palace and President Kennedy's sister Kathleen, who was married to the 10th Dukes's oldest son – the Marquis of Hartington. Both Kathleen and Billy Hartington, her husband, died in tragic circumstances.

There is plenty of car parking at Chatsworth and the house with its treasures should be allowed a couple of hours to wander around. Leaving via its large shop; the 106-acre (42.5 hectare) garden stretches away, with much to explore and excite you. You really need to allow a full day for your visit.

Set in the woods is an Adventure Playground and Farmyard for younger children, with lots of animals to see.

In spring, Stand Woods above and behind the house, reveal their beds of bluebells in full glory across the floor of the large wood, having reached the tall Elizabehan Hunting Tower. There are two large lakes above the valley and in Stand wood, that serve the Cascade and the Canal Pond.

The Painting Hall
(© Chatsworth House Trust, Peter Smith)

Chatsworth House, Bakewell, DE45 1PJ

☎ 01246 582204

www.chatsworth.org

Open: Daily, Easter to late-December; 11am-5.30pm

There is a restaurant, café and shop in the former stable block. At certain times there are popular behind-the-scenes tours well worth the visit, so telephone for information!

Chatsworth is also worth revisiting in December, for the Christmas lights.

Right: Peace Gardens

Below: Bath Gardens

Above: Queens Arms Inn (left) Peacock Inn (right)

Below: River Wye

Haddon Hall (*Courtesy of www.visitpeakdistrict.com*)

Haddon Hall

This venerable old house on the side of the A6 is about 2 miles (3.25km) on the south side of Bakewell. The car park is on the right hand side of the A6 and the house is across the road. The oldest part of the house is the chapel, partly built in 1080-90. The tour is through the lower part of the house, through kitchens, the banqueting hall, several adjacent rooms and the long gallery. The house was never altered over the centuries and many of the rooms are circa 500 years old.

The garden, small by Chatsworth standards, is non-the-less charming, with a memorable view down to a little packhorse-type bridge over the River Wye. There is a tea room and shop on site.

Haddon Hall, nr Bakewell, DE45 1LA

☎ 01629 812855 www.haddonhall.co.uk

Open: Daily, Apr-Sep, approx. 11am-5pm; Oct, Mon-Thursday 11am-5pm.

Lathkill Dale

This limestone dale is situated to the southwest of Bakewell. Ramblers combine a walk down the dale on a larger circular route, parking at Monyash or Over Haddon. If you want a stroll, leave Bakewell on the Monyash road. Take first left (Yeld Lane) and after leaving the residential area, carry on for about half a mile before turning right for Over Haddon. Park in the village car park and walk down the hill to the river. Walk upstream and then through the wooded section to a large mill pool (a former corn mill, Carter's Mill). The path is at the side of the river. After a break, return to the car. English Nature run the reserve here and their Visitor Centre is in Over Haddon. It is worth calling there before taking your walk up the dale.

Bakewell Tourist Information
Centre, Market Hall

Riverside walk, River Wye
(Image courtesy of www.visitpeakdistrict.com)

Attractions in Bakewell

Old House Museum

Cunningham Place, Off Church Lane, DE45 1DD
☎ 01629 813642
Folk museum in historic early sixteenth century house. Situated behind (and above) the church. Open: 11am-4pm daily, April-end of October.

M & C Collection of Historic Motorcycles

Off Matlock Street, DE45 1EF
☎ 01629 815011
Open: 11am-5pm on certain weekends in the summer. Telephone for details.

Attraction at Rowsley

Cauldwell's Mill & Craft Centre

Bakewell Road, Rowsley, DE4 2EB
☎ 01629 734374 (mill); 01629 733185 (craft centre)
Mill open: 10am-6pm, daily April-October; 10am-4.30pm November-March.
Historic water-powered flourmill, café, shop and craft centre.
Craft shop open daily all year.
Guided tours by arrangement (including evenings in summer).

ACCOMMODATION

Lists of various types of accommodation may be obtained from Tourist Information Centres. There is a full range of serviced accommodation: hotels, guest houses, bed & breakfast, farm houses, youth hostels, camp and caravan sites.

TOURIST INFORMATION CENTRE

Market Hall, Bridge Street, Bakewell

☎ 01629 816558 Fax: 01629814782

bakewell@peakdistrict.gov.uk

OTHER INFORMATION

Banks: Royal Bank of Scotland; Nat-West; HSBC and Halifax Building Society.

Market Day: Monday. A farmer's market is held on the last Saturday in the month, 9am–2pm at the Agricultural Centre – take the new bridge across the river from near the supermarket.

Recreation Ground: Matlock Road, between the A6 and the river on the south side of the town.

Swimming Pool: Granby Road ☎ 01629 814205

Golf: 9-hole/18-tee course. Visitors welcome. ☎ 01629 812307

Toilets: Granby Road, opposite the Police Station; the park; and the Agricultural Centre.

Published by **Ashbourne Editions**

Ashbourne Hall, Cokayne Ave, Ashbourne, Derbyshire, DE6 1EJ

Tel: (01335) 347349 Fax: (01335) 347303

1st edition: ISBN: 978-1-873-775-29-5

© **Stella Porter 2008**

Printed by: Gutenberg Press Ltd, Malta

Design by: Michelle Prost

Photography:

www.bakewellshow.org - 9 & 10

www.visitpeakdistrict.com - Front Cover, Back Cover Middle, 3 Bottom, 7, 11 Left, 13 Top Right & Bottom, 14, 15 Right

Mark Titterton - Back Cover Right, 4, 5 Left Top, 5 Left Bottom, 5 Bottom, 8, 11 Right, 13 Top Left

Chatsworth House Trust (www.chatsworth.org) - 12, Back Cover Main

All other images supplied by Lindsey Porter

Front Cover: View across the River Wye **Back cover top** (l-r): All Saints Church, The Original Bakewell Pudding Shop, Holme Bridge **Back cover main:** Chatsworth Garden